MOLT

by

Astrid Ferguson

ISBN: 0692068023
ISBN-13: 978-0692068021

DEDICATION

Someone Once said, "Others will see in us what we fail to see in ourselves…"
I would like to thank my husband, Jerel Ferguson aka @Jayreal215 on Instagram and Twitter, for inspiring me to write freely and for sketching the drawings found in this book. I love you and you're a wonderful artist

My high school teacher Teri Baller for pointing out grammatical errors and continuous support.
My family for being my greatest support system.
Last but not least my son's the double A's, for giving me the strength to do valiant things I never thought possible, just to see smiles on their faces.

Please follow me on the following social media sites:
Instagram: @astrid.ferg
Twitter: @ferg_astrid
Facebook Page Astrid Ferguson -Afergtale

As I stare into the desolate white scenery

I became trapped in thought

I traveled like the wind to a time I felt lost

It haunts my dreams

It prevents me from reaching

And shedding this negativity

I've tried prayer

I've tried meditation

I often write down these horrid dreams

Even still, my heart screams

I wake up in terror, sweat and tears

I am not sure I have a message the world wants to hear

I shake away my thoughts

I suppress those emotions

Until the day I woke up and decided a book is the tissue I need

CONTENTS

ACKNOWLEDGMENTS

To you reading these words

Walk a mile in my shoes

Feel the grace of my foes

Tear the tears I've shed

The blood I've bled

The feeling of being powerless and silenced by those you wished you'd forget

Forgetting the "who" and being replaced for "instead"

To demand respect of being viewed as queen by men

Only to get lost in the journey the thoughtless and greedy have led

Momentarily, then will you understand how womanhood sheds

Slough

Momma's Common Teachings

Solitude speaks louder in silence

It is not always welcomed to speak when you haven't been picked to do so, but you do it anyway

Vulnerability is counterproductive in the presence of oppression

Distrust is more loyal than trust

Beauty can only be held, admired and restored in different magnitudes

When it isn't measured, copied, bought or stripped from its originator

Voices can only be heard when everyone don't undermine the tones

Soften the tempos

Harmonize in phrases

We put down our torches

and forgive the torturers constant advances

Equality is defined in the dictionary

But it is misunderstood by many readers of vast categories

Freedoms can only be obtained when we find understanding,

We relinquish power,

We fail miserably when faced by voracity,

And lead by holding the hands in unison as momma said candidly

While standing in the kitchen during our cooking trainings

All things she wished she learned sooner and not just repeat

Mother was born in Dominican Republic, where she experienced great poverty. The kind that leads her to one of two options; Either marry to grow completely dependent on a man, or marry a US citizen so she can leave her motherland. My father was a citizen of the United States. Although he was born and raised in Haiti. To my mother's luck, he loved residing in Dominican Republic. There was something about mom that called dad's attention. At the time, my dad was good friends with my grandfather. Despite their 33 years gap a romance formed between my parents. Some would call it robbing the cradle, in Dominican Republic it was called "opportunity."

To make a long story short, they married and within a year or two of their marriage, I was born. My mother was age 19 and my father 52 at the time. When I turned one, my parents decided to venture off to the United States. They felt it was the only option to provide me with a better quality of life. That is when the real suffering began.

My parents did not see eye to eye. Their big age gap began to play tricks with their principles and sense of pride. My mother viewed my father as her savior. While my father tried teaching her education was a way of survival. He enrolled her in school and expected her to continue her education. He wasn't young and hip. He didn't own a car. As you can imagine, life was very boring for someone as young as my mother at the time.

My dad being, as frugal as he was, his idea of a date was taking my mom on a train ride from Manhattan to Brooklyn and back, without getting off. That is when he said, "This is New York!" Their marriage only lasted three years when they decided on a divorce. During the divorce proceedings, my mother met someone else, a Dominican like herself. He was young, he had swag, he had a car and moved around New York City well. Coming to the strange lands of America wasn't easy for her and he felt like the closest thing to home. To my mother's surprise she endured hunger, deceit, language barriers, physical and mental abuse while dating this new man. It just so happens he was "separated from his wife." As time went by and the divorce proceedings ended, my mother found out at eight months of pregnancy that my step-father was still seeing his wife. Big shocker, right? She had two children by this man. Things never got better. Instead, they got worse. In some twisted way, she felt her sacrifices and endurance were necessary so her children could have options to weigh. I know! I couldn't believe she convinced herself of this story.

Naturally, the same principles were being embedded in me. It was being instilled from a very young age how to become a wife before becoming a woman. I was taught to fold clothes, set the table, serve my step father in separate plates (not plastic). He must sit at the head of the table. If he demanded something to drink while everyone was eating, it was my mother's duty to get it for him. There were no intellectual conversations about my mother's dreams, hopes or aspirations. It was as if she didn't exist. She only coexisted when mentioned as his woman. The conversations were always about him and his choice of topics. So, it was then I realized, I was not supposed to exist independently without a man.

I was being nurtured to depend on a mans every need. I was being raised to become educated by attending school but not to voice my opinion. I had to learn to become kind but not assertive. I was to become frothy but not dense. I would not make a proper wife if I didn't learn early on how to fulfill my domestic duties while remaining silent. I was to believe everything the man promised me no questions asked. The lecture was the man, and he was to be viewed like the bible. He was the word and I was simply a disciple. Even if the promises came with lies and deceit. It was him who I was created for. I Astrid, was not complete unless his last name was tied to mine. I was to breed his children that will bare his last name. I am to feed his belly, keep his house clean, bow to his every command because it was my duty as his woman.

My mother was always outspoken and had a hard time biting her tongue, that is when he would beat her worse. It was evident she was miserable and dying inside before our very eyes. She was psychologically broken and lost her self-worth. She jumped from one man, who was vastly different from her, to another guy with whom she could relate, but didn't value her. Sometimes the things we want are not the things we need.

Daddy On the Line

I was too young to understand it all

It had been a few years since I'd seen my father

Just when I was beginning to think the man in our house was my father

The phone rings.

Taking a Seat at The Table

My vision

My hopes

My dreams, they weren't important once I left the school building

I was responsible for helping mother do dishes

Set the table, feed my siblings

It was my responsibility

It was my purpose

It was routine

Personal Translator

I had to travel in public transportation

Help mother extend her public benefits

In the public sector, we were a family of four not five

I learned math quickly constantly having to subtract and divide

I learned to lie to keep

Instead of telling the truth to be free

I was merely a dim candle in a big room full of bright lights

I didn't know wrong from right

I witnessed abuse and rape before my own eyes

Free Titles

Women from my culture were expected to fulfill wifely duties

Without being given both rings

His dreams

His plan

We were only along for the ride

Deceit, cheating, and drugs were just a part of everyday life

But I guess it was ok since mom had a legal job

She wasn't involved with any dealings

Little Girl Trapped in Grown Up Problems

I had no idea in my mind what a good guy would be like

My own father couldn't protect me from the man in the house

My step-father broke the windows of my mother's home

Until each one came crashing down

Making her hollow and weak

It was often at night when she would weep

Searching for answers in mirrors as her tears fell in the bathroom sink

He made her believe she would be nothing without him

He made her believe that his love was the only key

She loved him more than she loved me

He was her torturer holding the medicine and her remedy

Late Testimonies

Just like wolves hunting for sheep

He entered my room at night

He insisted on touching me

Running his fingers through areas between my navel and feet

For so long I couldn't sleep

I would hold my breath so no one could hear me

Mother never noticed

She never asked

She was a wounded pet

Too blind to see

She just stayed in silence

Praying for relief under the same seduction sheets he tried to enforce his masculinity

Can you notice?

Was it possible to create a voice while being afraid

How could I open doors when the keys were hidden

Could I describe a feeling when I didn't understand the language

Will they read my cries for help if I misspelled a word

If I used improper grammar

Would anyone care since my family didn't live in great walls of gold and grandeur

Did my story matter if it wasn't a popular action film, filled with well-known actors

Could I still be a princess if I dressed like a peasant

How could anyone notice me if I was a seed fed with unfiltered water

I lived in the hood of Manhattan, near the dirty concrete, large rats and filthy water

Often tried to make sense of who I was

Who I was intended to be

Did I matter to anyone in this great apple city

Would the world even care

I was only eleven wishing for a shining prince to come save me

I looked around and the life before me was foggy and unclear

My parent's foreigners who fought over custody and power

It was a battle of supremacy and inferiority

They say they were doing what was best for me

and I was too young to understand what was happening

The adults I lived with fought at night constantly

I went to school where my peers made fun of my clothes

They were either two sizes too big or knockoffs of popular brand names

It didn't matter that I was clean

Only what I was wearing wasn't the most popular thing

My father Haitian who looked more like my grandfather

My mother a Hispanic who knew very little English

I was beginning to hate the shameful feelings brewing

According to every statistic I read I was meant to be pregnant by 16

I was intended to fall for some vagabond that would abuse and mistreat me

It was the norm to be someone's woman and not their queen

I would only be following mothers lead

My mother could not help me with my homework

My father was too far to attend any school meetings

The excuse was his sickness didn't allow long travels, he lived in Brooklyn

My mother had house chores and two other children to feed

She also had a man she must accommodate, she had enough to keep her busy

Fathers your daughters are in desperate need

They are being left behind like sheep

The wolves are taking over her keep

She is being fed scraps of meat

Daughters are no longer being viewed as majestic and gentle creatures

These vultures are more interested in her features

Your absence is most felt at night when she pleads

Mom, I needed Daddy here not his money

Be careful of the advice you give her

Little girls learn from the sights they see

Even if you're there in physicality

How you treat her and the company you keep

Will be the treatment she will accept mentally

Train Rides

This is the part where we converse, indirectly. Have you ever been to New York City? Have you ever traveled by train? Well in New York City the subway experience will always stick out in your mind. I'm not sure if it's the crowd or the vast performances you experience, for free. There is something about people just sitting next to each other regardless of financial status, race or gender. Just a total stranger that you may meet again later in your life. Then again, you may not. What I do know, is that as a little girl, I knew the train ride was where I was mostly at peace.

Friday, you are here

You finally came to save me

Three pm

The bell rings

Daddy stands outside the school building

Straw hat, black slacks, dressy shoes with metal taps

He always stood out in any crowd

Smiling in relief it's time for our weekend train ride

 Manhattan to Brooklyn it's my weekend getaway

There is something soothing and peaceful about iron wheels turning and gliding on the railway

The screeching sounds of the train moving in fast motions

Makes you think of waves and oceans

With each stop

Each station you look out the windows

You see new faces

Every face except the face of beast you hate to see every day

Oh, how I wished I could take this ride every day

Not even daddy knew the hell I was living

Empty Seat

Behind the windowpane

She stands staring into space

Washing dirty dishes

Fulfilling the long list of chores

To fill an empty fridge, she returns to the grocery store

She cooks dinner for him

She washes his laundry

She dries off the sheets

She prepares the house for his grand entry

She is tired

Her back and feet aches

But she doesn't complain

She must find her second wind

It is her body tonight he wants to claim

She prepares to listen to his dreadful office stories

She must not interrupt

She must refrain

The urge of sharing her very own thoughts

be still, serene, simple and plain

Clean up the table

Wash the kids' faces and hands

Tuck them into bed once again

Sort their clothes by name

Read them a fairy tale story

Their favorite about a princess and her prince, that will fight for her defense

Diminish sounds

Silence any voices that remain

Turn off the lights, he's had a long day

short conversations will suffice for today

Sit in your chair

Preparing for the same routine as yesterday

Make him breakfast

Iron his clothes for the workplace

It's what good wife economics meant in the 1950's

I read about it back in the day

Lady of the house only means

You accompany him on the plane

You are merely a passenger

Who rides alongside in cars under his name

An extra luggage he carries to fulfill his domain

If another woman catches his eye

He stares and makes her feel inferior and insane

He may have a few flings

In his phone, he stores away

But if he returns home she'll continue to stay

For reasons only her mind entertains

At night when he touches her

It doesn't feel the same

She stares up at the ceiling

Wondering if he even remembers her real name

Money and Power

Money can provide a man with two options

The opportunity to provide for his family

Or

The power to humiliate and dismantle

The authenticity, humility, and the most caring soul of a woman

Moving Walls

It seemed like every year the concrete walls changed like seasons

I wasn't in a place long enough to make good friends

Before the moving truck showed up again and again

This time it was time to leave New York City

A new word invented for Different, "Disorder"

In a world where everyone is supposed to move at the same beat of a drum

Walk on the same leg like a marching band

Sing on the same tune like a chorus

Your brain waves are expected to interconnect with neurons of your neighbors

Reflections resemble shadows of what's considered "normal"

If you have a nose, two eyes, one mouth and a face

That doesn't make you humanly worthy of acceptance

It just makes you resemble one

If you stomp your feet when everyone runs

If you shout while everyone sings

If learning ability is a few grades behind from him, her and/or the whole damn body of people who took the fucking survey, exam

You are not different

You are a disorder the system throws in a suitcase

A disorder used in a loose phrase so we can diagnose you with prescriptions of hate

I say we because even I find myself questioning if I am the definition of normal

sometimes, maybe I also need prescriptions for life pains

Your name rides in brief cases

To drawers

To filing cabinets

To principles offices

To doctors appointments

To court dates

Only to be stamped "disorder"

A liability this nation can't take

A world where your shadow runs away like a vagabond when the sun shines on it's face

Your vision blurs when faces invade your space

You've been rejected by everyone who thinks the same

You relinquish getting close to someone because you have accepted you're a burnt bulb in a bright place

When all this time you were just different

You simply coped with Life in a different way

Maybe you were normal and everyone else was the disorder manufactured and prepackaged the same

You are a brilliant reward to touch the earth's surface

We just simply have too much pride believing you are worth loving all the same

I'm not saying I'm normal or I am better than the person you hate

I am just saying I understand

I can relate

I'm more comfortable sitting in the dark then standing on stage in a crowded place

Prisoner

Held captive by lack of knowledge

Lack of courage

And strong pigmentation

Prisoner to societies political anomalies

So are the statements they make to shelter the chosen

Feet pace slowly

Pushing forward to seek keys

With every foot planted something new grows preventing us to exceed

Still we proceed

But held prisoner by sacrifices for our families

The chains get heavier

They extend and develop new demons to bob and weave

But still I walk against the grain

Striving, improvising but held

Prisoner to the mental estate of wanting to be great

As dreams turn into nightmares before I obtain

Winning is not an option before losing to strain

Stripped of every ounce of possibility

Prisoner to oppression of thy ancestors before they were trained

Still I continue in hope

In faith

In the belief that it's better to be prisoner

To my own fantasies

Then to be held captive to someone else's foundation

Sustained by gravity of complacencies

Deeply coiled

Deeply sunken with the knowledge of speech

Lies corruption of tongue that makes it harder to breathe

If it is meant to never speak

To never dream

To never follow the sunbeams

Prisoner to you lord and not man I shall be

For you guide the purpose

You guide the speed

I'm simply a prisoner trying to break free

Not knowing who you were

Who you are now

And who you plan to become in the future

Is the reason you're unable to molt

Molting is the process of shedding

Skin

Nails

Layers of yourself

Allowing space for new growth

After-all, all butterflies were once caterpillars encaged cocoons

With a frame thin as a thread

A face with large nostrils

I wasn't the most attractive teenager in high school

Mother would say eat more loafs of bread

Father would suggest playing a sport

At family gatherings everyone would comment on my thin display

Once I gained weight my family said

Lose some weight if a husband is what you want to catch

No one said you look beautiful today

Learning to Forgive

Things were bad huh? I know that's what you're thinking. To any girls and boys out there hating home, please know life won't always be this way. I know it sounds like shit! I know I sound like every other person that you've tried to talk to. But Let me tell you this, I was once in your shoes. Although, you may not understand now, you will have to forgive those who have hurt you the most. Even if it is your own mother. Sometimes, we fail to see the bigger picture. We get lost in the now and never look beyond our windows. My mother wasn't a bad mother. She gave me all she could. She even sacrificed her better life thinking she was doing the right thing. She had good intentions. I'd like to think most of us moms do. So whatever pain is keeping you from outgrowing the painful shells of childhood, let it go. It's a weight too heavy to carry forever.

For you to bloom your mother had to plant roots

She may not always be right

but her only intention is to water your growth

Light enters the room

As the drops of water collect on the windows

Just another dreary school day

As mother enters the room shouting

Wake up kids

To her surprise

She is lifted by her t-shirt

Across our dresser

Landing on the ground

Rain drops with blood clusters begin to collect on her face

Defeat

With love as my counterpart

Happiness as my struggle

Pain is my preamble

I'm collected in many stories

Begin to form narratives

Carefully noticing

Impassive will become your name

I'm admired by most

Enemies serve me with toast

With friends disguised as close folks

Champagne, failure is the celebration I chose

Drawn to me like a puppy to lactose

Insecurities surface afloat

Simply inviting me to save them a loaf

I'm always the topic chosen by those you hated most

I'm always spoken about

Never directly spoken to

It is them versus me the topic

With most ratings and reviews

I remain lurking in the veins

Resembling IV's with purpose and servitude

How long I stay depends on your attitude

Routine

Your husband calls when he forgets activities

The kids only notice you by the apron you keep

You are not thy enemy, it is I.

If I shelter my voice,

Forget thy pride,

Lose my inner peace,

Drop my gloves in the dirt,

I've accepted being broken

I will shatter into pieces that you will only use as tokens

I will be lost in the universe but turned into stone once spoken

You will not see the female you've chosen

You will only see a sketch of a dying person

Failure in my bosom I will feed future generations fast and frozen

Empathy will be like a description crossed off by rags with detergent

Popular Girl

You are the umbrella

I always forgot on rainy days

I walked hallways

Drenched in unpopularity every teenaged day

While you stayed dry

Befriending girls that forgot you on graduation day

Don't judge a book by its cover they say

Unfortunately, its human nature to allow the first impression

To make an everlasting one

Framed degrees hung on walls

doesn't make you brilliant

It makes you educated

Strong Legs

You know you've reached a whole new level of strength

When you look Evil in the eyes and say, "Hi"

While still feeling your legs

Self-Love

Love can become your refuge

Love can be worn as armor

It can also cut life a sword

It's the air your lungs need to breathe to work at maximum capacity

But once gone it can suffocate you instantly

It's the medicine

It's the antidote

But first you must learn to be steady

You must learn to float

#WCW

We constantly seek affirmation

We constantly dwell on acceptance

We diminish our dreams and aspirations

By living in constant fear of rejection

We devalue our talents and stump on our progression

Simply because the world may not agree with our creations

Change the rules

Change the scenery

There is no set way or form to creativity

Adjust your focus

Zoom in your lens

See your vision

And capture the beauty of your homeland

Artistry can be read

Can be felt

By image or pen

Find your hidden talents and paint them in colors bold with intent

Woman, you are all you need

You are a flower

You will bloom

Even through the cracks of concrete

Your stems grew

You don't have to know everything to glow

But you must water your earth to prevent stunt growth

Simply remain confident and wear your thrown

Don't ponder about things, people, or past thorns

Live freely

Seek inner peace continuously

to live happily

Never abandon your dreams

because someone living their nightmare told you so

Anything easy is never good

Anything good is never easy

Baking without Rules

Lay the flour

Roll out the dough

Evenly as possible

Take your cookie cutter

Cut out even portions

Perfect, just like the recipe

You chose a place that resembles your neighbors

Quiet and pristine community

White walls

Hardwood floors

Granite countertops

It looks like a page in a magazine

Holidays

Seasons

Every size and shape

There's a cookie cutter with the perfect frame

Except human

You can't find it in any store isle

You decide to skip the cookie cutter

You begin to form your own shape

It isn't perfect

It isn't great

It doesn't even look like the picture on the magazine page

It was a free hand shape that looks like SHIT!

But guess what

It tastes just as great

Do not waste time on jealousy

Sometimes you're ahead

Sometimes you're behind

The race is long and everyone has a different stopwatch

Respect those who finished before you and encourage those who follow behind you

The hardest prison to escape is your mind…

Letting it Air Out

Detaching the lids of sealed tight containers are necessary

Everything needs to air out

Releasing those air bubbles, we've stored

That keeps us tasting like sour lemons

Asthmatic

Imagine if something as organic as laughing too much could cost you your last breath

If playing tag with your friends could send you on a stretcher to the ER

If being outside doing some gardening could end up with someone else shoveling a hole for your coffin

If you can imagine for a quick second what that would feel like

you could relate to all of us suffocating in this life who appear different on the surface

We are all asthmatics with lungs longing for more oxygen called kindness

Focus

I dislike the saying "I'm gonna do this or I'm gonna do that"

I don't want to hear about what you plan to do

You're trying to convince yourself of your plans

No one talks about stepping on the gas before reaching their destination, they simply drive there

Take the wheel and stop questioning if you can do it

Just do it!

As humans, we constantly worry about what we wish we had

or the things we want

Through this course of action, we forget about cherishing what we have

We don't appreciate the virtues we have been blessed with

Stop worrying about the end, start at the beginning

Ungrateful I(we) Are

I am like a fish in the dream water of heaven

asking God for wings to fly to the sun

to breathe the scent of flower.

I am like an eagle flying alone

wishing to walk on mountains.

I'm a human asking for miracles to change

my coloring.

Keep your gears in drive

Not in reverse

If you make a conscious decision to reverse

Make sure it's the only way to go forward

Not all relationships are based on lies and deceit

Not all separations result in heartaches

Broken people

And cold sad sheets

Sometimes you must learn to walk on your own two feet

You know,

Move at your own speed

Not every failed friendship contained a villain

Not every failed relationship had a damsel in distress

Sometimes it's merely your time was on a different time zone

And you couldn't meet at the breakeven point

Sharing is Caring

We all go through our own tragedies

Often, we hold on to them as sworn secrecies

This mentality begins to eat away at our souls and prevent us from blooming

Sharing your story can set you free and at the same time help someone else see more clearly

Stay curious it keeps the mind working at maximum capacity

Home

is not four walls

the address you write on the top left-hand side of an envelope

That is only a tangible description of where you currently reside

Home encapsulates so much more of the intangible things often taken for granted

Running Towards Something

Jump like a grasshopper

Pull like an angry gorilla

Push through the pain like limbs in ice water

Dig deep

Fight your greatest enemy "Self"

Only to look up and see the finish line pushed out further

Shedding Shells

Letter to Young Me

You have been through many trials. Many of which have left your self-esteem fragile and weak. You will be loved because you are worth loving. You may not look like a model, you are very skinny. So what? Embrace your appearance, your imperfections make you beautiful. There are so many women that in their adult lives wish they looked like you. Don't allow the immaturity of those around you fool you.

You will one day marry. You will one day have children of your own. Currently, just enjoy loving yourself. You have been too busy doing everything for everyone else. It's time you walked the world with confidence. Let go of those bitter moments from your past childhood days. Forgive your mother for not knowing better at the time. She didn't mean to hurt you. In fact, she had no idea she was. She will also one day move on. She won't change her ways but just let God deal with her on his timing. It is not your weight to carry.

Every failed relationship you will have are lessons learned. It will make you wiser, stronger so you never have to settle for less than you deserve. For some guys, you will be too much and that is alright. Just remember it is not worth deflating yourself to meet their expectations.

It is ok to choose to go to college and get a degree before having children. It is ok to postpone growing a family until you are ready. It is ok to say, "I want MORE out of life." It is ok to want to marry and not just co-exist with someone. Is ok to want to be more than some man's child's mother. Most of all, through every testimony you will be OK. Walk quickly but not in a hurry. You will reach every goal you set. I promise you...

Sincerely,

Older You

Wake Up Call

Reminiscing about the past is like snoozing your alarm clock

So that you can never wake up just in time

Love for the Bad Boys

I was an old soul roaming campus

I wasn't focused on parties and boys

Concentrated on the sky

He came along with young, wild intentions

I wanted to break the mold of always following recipes

He crossed off every tradition

And burnt anything we could create

I was left an old soul with burnt toast on my plate

Virginity

He looked at me with staring eyes

My time was up

He wanted his prize

My mouth felt dry

Cotton balls collected in my throat

Silence and fear filled my lungs

He pulled the sheets

He didn't allow me to screech

Not this time

Waiting three years was too long

He wasn't letting me leave

He kicked down the door

He demanded I let him inside

He didn't want to wait

I wasn't ready

I can't believe I would lose my virginity this way

Selfish…

A man will see potential in you

But he's not ready to commit

So, he'll give you only half of himself

He'll string you along like a puppet

Wave fake promises he doesn't intend to worship

When all along he knew he wanted something different

I miss you

Scrolling through my phone for pictures of us

Reliving moments in my mind

Replaying voice mails just to hear your voice

One last time

I rather be dreaming with you

Then

Awake without you

I keep replaying yesterdays in my mind

I can't move on

I suppress accepting you're gone with ocean waves

That you are traveling with the winds of Manhattan

I feel divided

    Ashamed

I didn't do all I could to keep you

To show you I love you

I didn't run fast enough to say good-bye

You left me

My first love

I can't believe you're gone

Now all I have left of you is this briefcase of letters

One day we'll meet again

I just wanted you to know I miss you and I'll never forget you

When Two Strange Souls Meet and Mirror Secret Voids

I'd like to think that you and I Collided

    like water and land

I'd like to believe that I left traces in your mind

    like oceans on sand

I'd like to feel we have a mutual understanding

    like blue skies on sunny days

I'd like to leave knowing that we may not be the same but we respect each other

    like stars evenly spaced on the nightly gaze

Wrong Prescription (Bad Sex)

I was in so much pain and seeing you was like seeing a bottle of Aleve

I drunk your pills and washed you down with a glass of milk

To only realize you were a vitamin placed in a white bottle with the label Aleve

You weren't medicine

You weren't even a short relief

You were a poor excuse of me believing I needed someone to want me

Wrath

You forgot I had options

You made me weight them shits

You were thirsty, looking for juice in chicks with Chanel lipsticks

Luxury shoes

They were easy pickings

You would come home late as shit

Making up excuses not to pick up your kid

I made you think

I was ride or die while I plotted my exit

You thought I was a stupid bitch

Here are your keys

Bills and empty place

Now you feel lonely and think I care about your "I miss you" texts

Now you're the bitch in training

Excuse me

New guy is calling

His name is NEW DICK

If you're a vegetarian don't dine with someone who only brings beef to the table

Heavy Thoughts

In silence

Is when the weight gets heavy

In silence

Is when the real heavy lifting begins

In silence

Is when the most listening occurs

Laziness is the most common trait found in people who are complacent with dissatisfaction

Everything that person could ever broadcast are added excuses

Don't allow these individuals excuses to become your reasoning for conveniently staying dissatisfied

Trust me I was stuck there for more than half my short life

All these life lessons learned and I'm still the first person to tell myself
"You're not good enough…Yet"

Cheap Voyages

Books served as first class flights I could afford

Words described destinations I couldn't see outside my window

My pen suited as the therapist I could call 24/7

Diaries held stories I would recite in the dark corners of my twin size bed

My pillows were my stage

The alarm clock was my audience saying, "hurry, you need to wrap this up."

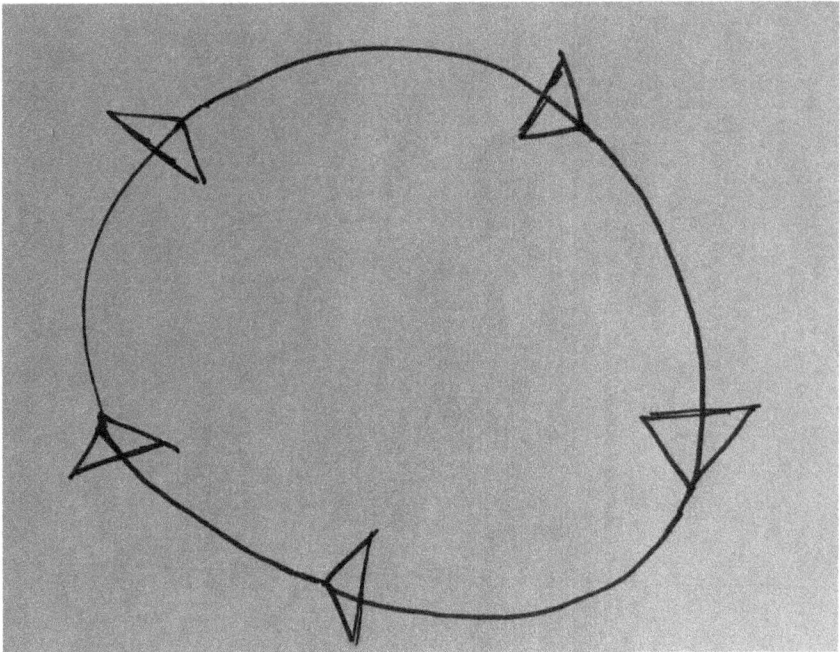

Dating is a journey

It's an adventure

It's about discovery

It's a series of episodes and experiences

They are not your mistakes

They're past, present and future checklists

That you scan on occasion with a glass of wine

It's going places and trying new things

Laughter and tears

Stress and facing fears

They're like growing pains

Outgrowing people

And remaining the same

He's not the One

When a man says, "You can do better than me."

You should listen

Don't try to prove him wrong

Don't try to change his mind

Just cut your losses and pray peace he will find

By staying,

him you will blame

For not giving you the love you exclaim

Despite his warnings

You decided to remain

He warned you without revealing

He is a boy in search of healing

You may dream of becoming his wife

Carrying his baby

But if he isn't ready

You will be left empty

He will cut you deep

He will cause you pain

He cares enough about you to say refrain

I know you think you see potential

You think you saw something overlooked by plenty

While you may be correct

or just insane

Save your energy, body and fairytale fantasy

Settling

He can offer you a white horse and carriage

He can buy you Fendi

Materially he has amply

Wallets full of money

Pockets overflowing

Can he offer you peace?

Can he offer you a chance of growing?

Together twenty plus years will he always choose you over many?

Can he offer you loyalty?

Jewelry full of bling, shiny and heavy

Can he make you priority?

Not just escort you as temporary

Can he build with you?

Do more tricks than just turn you on your belly

Can he teach you lessons?

Not leave you with a lesson to learn

If he cannot provide you with love you deserve

You will be with someone but remain alone

Mr. Right vs. Mr. Right Now

Mr. Right Now is only interested in sufficing your current symptoms

Mr. Right is interested in curing your lifelong brokenness and becoming your lifelong remedy

Choose wisely or end up in a life-long cycle of unhappy diseases.

There's a new bitch in town

She's known in the streets

She's talked about globally

She slides in DM's and retweets

She floods the visual gates of every man she meets

She has a phat ass

Thin waist

Pretty face

And a phat kitty

She appears to be perfection

She's every guys Wednesday crush

She wears luxury shoes, cool shades and carries a mean clutch

She's the only girl I know that gets constant press

She's the envy of the town

She wins every contest

She's the girl you love to hate but follow her every footstep

She goes by many names

Depending on which button you press

But she's mostly known as social media, ask your man how many likes and follows she gets

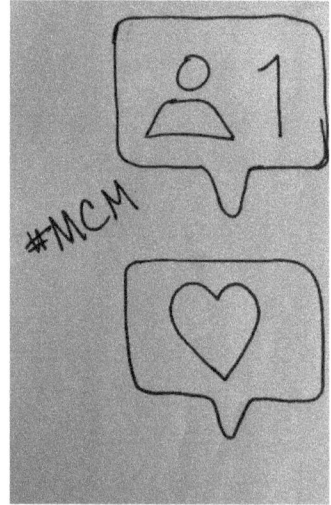

Don't be fooled by the monetary

Sometimes the guy with the largest bag of coins has the least offering

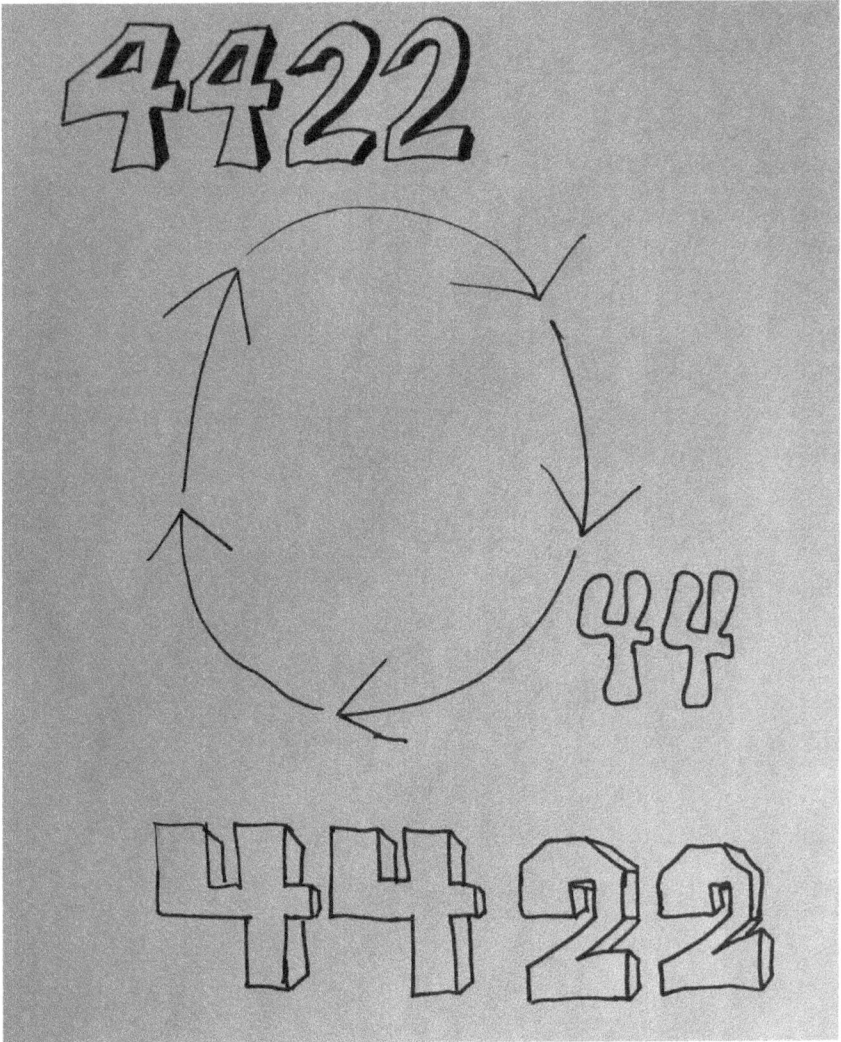

If you're a vegetarian

Don't dine with someone

Who only brings beef to the table

Insecurity floats

How confident you sway

I can careless about your visual display

No matter how many travels your way

Healing is not part of this contractual inlay

See I never show up just once

I may repeat in amplitude

But what is certain is that everyone

Will send me an invitation

When they miscalculate latitude and longitude

I am misunderstood by many

As exposure is trending

No matter the age, religion, gender or race

I accept all applications

I do not discriminate

I assist your deep sunken fears

I misdirect your opportunities to reverse gear

I misconstrue your plans from reach to nowhere

I am what others enjoy inflating

Simply because I am close enough to relate

I have been drawn by the most polished as portrait

Painted by colors that eyes admire to translate

I am the eluded trait

That sits next to frustrate

I may leave

I may stay

I'll always be lurking between your mind and every heartache.

Moonlight

Shine your light on my pillow sheets

Fill the gap he left for me to weep

Soothe my soul from the taste of bittersweet

I gave him all of me

He shattered me into pieces

I must now find the strength to sweep

I know I am worthy

I know my flesh is weak

Wipe away his scent

Erase his name from my memory

I don't want to feel hollow

Or empty

I'm tired of this apathy coiled deep

I want to remember how to smile

And accept we are history

Love

I often dreamt about you

I often inquired about you

I often thought I found you

Just as often I was left lost and empty-handed around you

I was lifted in a graceful yet subtle manner by your carbon copy

I was elevated to what I thought felt like you

Only to be cut loose at slight elevation by an emotion that emulated you

I started to curse you, damn you, and quite honestly

hate you

I was devastated and torn to pieces by what I thought it meant to have you

Often questioning if you existed or you were just fecal matter powdered with rose petals

I guess the farther into the abyss of sadness

Loneliness and disappointment

I fell into the laps of realization

I wasn't ready or educated enough to have you

I only cared for what felt good about you

What mattered is what felt astonishing

Never did I once care enough to understand everything about you

Never did it dawn on me that you too Love have been starved and stricken by others who did not worship you

Others did not worship your feelings, your unity, your ability to crush the hearts of those who are blinded to see every detail about you

Details of how you too have been lost

You too have been set aside for lust

You too have been forgotten by those who claim to love you most

That you the most powerful force

Emotion, feeling that can unite kingdoms, birth children, nurture all living things

represent every color,

handle every brushstroke

and blend perfectly as colorful colorless canvas have simply been framed on a wall

Stenciled on a card and caged in some fantasy

You have been relinquished to a good read, a good quote, a reference point used for deliberation

I did not understand you Love

I did not know that Love also had cloudy skies

I did not know that you Love contained many layers waiting to be peeled

Layers to be carefully handled

Gently felt to find the true blessing of your purest truth

I did not know that all those times I was rejected

I was being redirected

I was only being pulled closer to the true carrier of love

I apologize for not being more delicate with you sooner

for not gracefully accepting you earlier

for not embracing your gentle and warm embraces

for not healing your scars and admiring your battle wounds

I am finally ready for you love

I am finally openly, psychologically, spiritually and physically ready for you love

I have finally found that you reside within me, love

You reside within all living things, love

We just haven't learned to move something's around to allow you to grow faster than hate my love

It's not about the time

Or price tag

It's the fact I occupied some of your mental space

Sad Truths

It's easier to lay in misery

And cover myself in blankets of lies

To profess I am fine

It is how I shield how I am really doing inside

Admittance to being broken

Is surrendering to being desperate

In constant searches for a guide

See its harder to be vulnerable then be guarded by pride

Some of us remain strong because we enlighten our minds

Others like me, remain strong by building the shell you see before your own eyes

I may never admit to you how broken I am inside

For me it's a type of protection at this current time

If I allow you to enter

Without knowing if you're just visiting for a short time

And permit you to venture my insides

I have supplied you with keys to enter my mental design

MOLT

You will find your way to my heart

And there you'll reside

Without signing a contract before saying goodbye

So, let me die slowly within the corners of your eyes

For this is the sad truth why we lie, to each other, you and I

It's not always your fault

Sometimes

I just make a mess out of nothing

Go back to taking your time

Our fingers travel globally in seconds

Our palms have first class seats and infinite mileage points

Everything is fast

In a hurry

And who can do it first

Falling astray from working hard

Building life one brick at a time

Our lives, relationships, and successes with patience

Is outweighed by our level of expectations

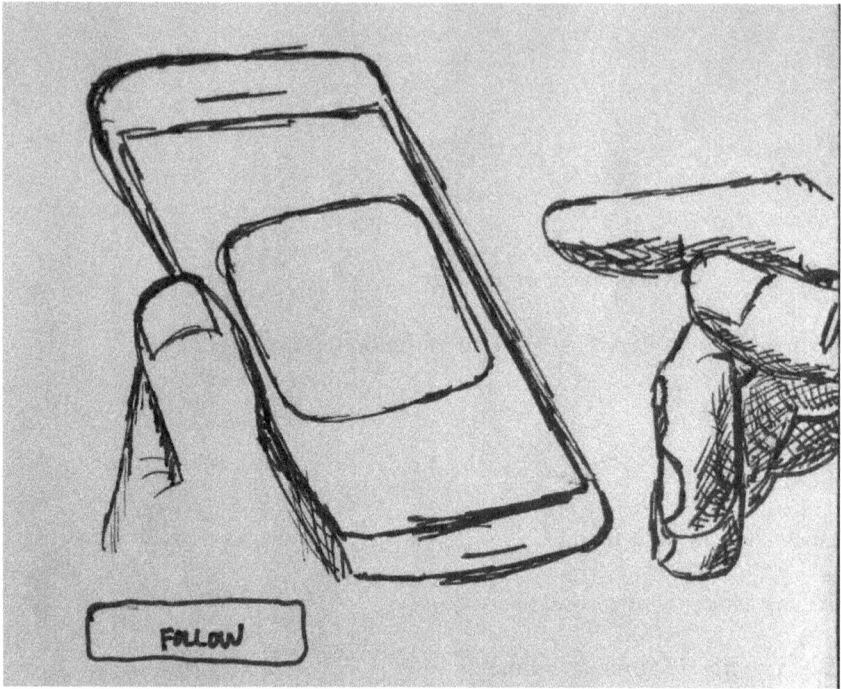

He felt like spring

A seldom touch

Wet my lips

Whispered through my hair

Yanked onto my skin

He felt like summer

Flushing my moist thoughts

With fingers rough as sand paper

He felt like autumn

Limbs like branches

I held me like leafs

He felt like winter

I've awakened in cold loss

Seeing nothing but my breathe every lonely morning

Solitude doesn't mean something is wrong with you

It simply means you are exactly where you should be…

Breaking

Exiting

Loving

Innovating

Entering

Valuing

evolving into an **I**nnermost **N**ew **G**rander version of yourself

Smile wider

Wear it like your scarf

It'll keep everyone confused

Outer Layer

From One Adult to Another

Life takes us in directions we don't always pin on maps. Sometimes they don't even appear on the grid. The location doesn't matter. What matters is knowing there is always more than one exit. In this part of the book things will get a little heavy. You see things differently when you are now responsible for another life. Everything you thought you knew gets turned upside down. Your life takes a back seat and this little person is now the wheel. When you are little you can easily blame your parents for your shortcomings and successes. The day when you become a parent yourself is when you realize how hard it really is to guide someone else, when you need guidance yourself.

I am no saint. I am not a preacher. I don't have the answers to many questions or situations. I just wish I knew better during the times of hardships. I wish I'd paid closer attention to the signs that were being waved in front of me. Just about every woman dreams of one day marrying and having children of her own. Never in her dreams is there a part about her raising a child on her own. In the dreams of marriage, you think of princess and prince fairy tale stories. Many women have their perfect ring picked out in their minds. They have the ceremony cut out from magazines. Some even have a dream dress.

A man however, thinks differently. He is more concerned on building first. Fun is the first thing on his itinerary. Marriage is usually the last thing on his list. Most men not all, will listen to their friends and show off for their friends before they do for their girl-friends. They will say they don't get caught up on titles. Forgetting titles is what we live for. We like having extra letters next to our names. We like placing name tags and dates. Some of us like the name tags on the clothes we wear. Titles are everywhere.

I will share a few things I wish I'd known then. Before you decide to give someone the greatest gift, which is life, be sure to be certain that person has earned it. No, not that you love him and he loves you. No, not he has money to provide for you and his child. Love is not enough when it comes to bearing children. Money is never enough for all the child expenses. Do all your research. Pay close attention to how he treats his mother. The woman who gave him life. That will tell you how he would treat you as his wife. Watch closely how he handles hard situations. Does he run? Does he make up excuses? Does he get mad and punch a wall? Does he face them without fearing any outcomes? Is he willing to lose everything for doing what is right?

If you can't answer those questions or if you can, but the answers do not align with your expectations, run. Run as fast as your feet can take you. This is also a question for the men. If she is not worthy of being your soulmate then why make her the mother of your greatest creation? Be more selective about who you chose as the mother of your children. It can be a life or death situation. With adulthood comes responsibility. With responsibility comes many sacrifices, hard decisions, risks, and hardships. Accept any mistakes you've made and make the best out of what you have in hand.

The Universe is constantly giving us signs

We just never read them

Because we're too busy driving

Scrolling through social media

Woman to Woman

You have made some mistakes. You have kissed a few frogs along the way. You find yourself lonely at times. This feeling sometimes makes you cave and accept things you shouldn't. You have lost yourself along your adulthood journey. That is ok. You are going through everything you were intended to go through. Every pain you have felt, every broken heartache, every disappointment, every rejection, every failed attempt, every victory, every step was necessary.

You are evolving into a grown ass woman. It doesn't matter how many times you fall. What matters is that you pick yourself back up every time. Your mistakes don't make you a bad person or a worse option. They make you a better person and the top tier option because you have survived. If he doesn't want you someone else will. DO NOT SETTLE.

New things can feel overwhelming...

At first

It can feel a bit discouraging

They can make you question if you're capable

If you're doing the right thing

It is a pony ride with a joker in a bad circus ride living in your mind

You will get stuck in the middle of

Do I jump and possibly sink?

Or

Do I stay and drown in what if's?

Shaking The Excess

Pulling back the hoods of the dark black cloaks

removing layers of weight

imitating featherlike piles

I allow the wind to travel my every being

Take me to the sun

show me how to kneel in the presence of humbleness, once again

Remind me to check on my neighbor

Find a compelling compassion I've lost through material gain

Guide me to being human once again

It is the only way I can shake this longing excess

Hope Amongst the Stars

Arithmetic, algorithms we learn to solve

Theories we construct

Buildings, professions, creativity become part of our name tags

We visualize growth of our monetary seeds

But

We forget to fertilize our daily needs

We become blind mice

Losing the ability to view ourselves in one another

We place power on Forbes financial worth ratings

We form excuses to accept less

Then

We turn into paperclips as one looking into the atmosphere

All the same

With wondering eyes full of hope

Asking the stars for the same thing "Compassion"

I am Sazon con Griyo

I am blended with mangu and creole

I am the result of my ancestors dancing merengue and kompa

When I walk my hips sway with the sounds of drums and trumpets

I curve like Spanish guitars

My tongue rolls perfect R's

I am the encapsulated result of island love

Hispañola island where waves turn and splash in celebration

Where the color of flesh are all different shades

Where the palm trees stand tall like kings

I am MI Tierra Isla Bonita

Dominican Skin

My skin is the first thing you see

I wear it proud, unapologetically

It is both a gift and a curse

Everyone assumes my story

In every country racism runs free

We use it to divide and judge those we meet

Black is a term of endearment in my Hispanic language

Ironically, it is not the color preferred by the wealthy

As Dominicans, we come in many shades

We were mixed with so many cultures across our seas

We were intertwined and mingled with dictatorship, broke, rich, slavery and everything in between

We are not even considered Spanish even though they played a part in our history

Still we sit and judge those who live next to you and me

It is the greatest ignorance to keep believing these old common teachings

See the beauty of my people is that we are not just one thing

We are Latinos who love to dance and drink President when we get thirsty

Being poor is just minor to say the least

When you have a neighborhood unity

We will modestly give you anything within reach

I love my country!

I love my color

Many pay for tans so they can look like me

I will never pretend to fit where I am misunderstood

I speak two languages, I could have spoken three

I should be able to communicate with you better, but you were too busy judging me

Dominicans are known for working in factories

They own salons they own many things

They get picked apart by society because they look at you differently

We left our motherland for something grand and sweet

But still we preserve our heritage

Come have dinner with us, we're eating rice and beans

Haiti

You are the love I never met

I've heard you speak

I've tasted your seasonings

I know about you but haven't seen you face to face

I see your beauties in pictures

My father often brought you up in conversations

I know you have a long history

While I have never met you personally you are a part of me

I am…

I am not one thing

I am not all things

I am fruitful and sweet

I am bitter but fragile

I am tender and rare

I am serenity, insanity, elusive, and can lead you to prosperity

I am not one color

I am not every color

I am not one race

I am not all races

I can't be described as just this

Or that

I am not for debate

I am who I am and will always remain

I am not her, you or some
fantasy

I am Madame

I am Señorita

I am princess

I am my own Queen

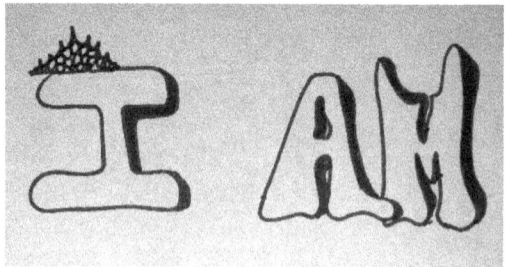

Questioning Everything

I tolerated your lies

Your constant back stabbing empty words

I endured being broken

I believed in us more than I believed in myself

On paper you fit the perfect description

No criminal record

No prior children

College educated

Legally employed

Tall, Confident

Well dressed

Apparently, you were what every woman dreamed

As we became a growing couple I realized

I couldn't catch my breath

I wasn't alive

I was just living beside you

I was trying to stake a post in the sand

I wasn't cultivating my best life

So why are we together?

Oh yea

There is a child in the next room

Single Mother

He split me open like a watermelon

Sucking up my sweetness

& leaving only his seeds

One Sprouted

Growing vastly

With skin light as sand

He wasn't colorful enough

So we were both rejected

From forming a happy family

Trust is hard to give because we fear

Returning to prisons of growing pains

The brutal beatings of knowing better

Ink My Strength

In tight corners

    lonely in silence

with a pen in my hand

    is where I'm my strongest

Parenting 101

There is no standard order of procedures

There is no exact manual

There's no magical guide

There isn't an exact science or written policies

You simply do the best you can with what you have

When you are a single parent you are everything to your child. You are the mom and the dad. You have added pressure to make shit work. You don't have another person to call when things get tough. You can't just get up and go have a drink. The other parent if they are involved in any way, doesn't really see things your way. Sometimes they barely even see their own children. If you can co-parent it will make things easier for your child. If you can't the child is who will hurt the most. Don't lose sight of who matters most even when arguments feud.

There is something disheartening when you see your child missing out on plenty of things, because you must work two jobs to pay bills and feed him. I will never forget how guilty I felt for not being able to provide my son with his dream of having his mommy and daddy together. He had no idea of how much I had to fight just for his existence. Relationships are always swell and smooth until you throw a child into the mix. If you love your child and you are willing to do whatever is necessary, please don't feel guilty about what you can't give them. You will have dark nights. You will go hungry to provide for them. You will have to fight demons just to make your lives better. But guess what? It is all worth it.

To any single mothers and fathers out there simply trying to make it, you are so appreciated. Your hard work will not go unseen. Your prayers are being heard. Keep fighting for what you deserve. Your child is not a mistake. You are not a mistake. You just need a break. It is coming, don't you worry. Just don't give up. Don't give up hope.

Mail

Morning

Another day has gone by

Sip on some tea

Check your schedule

Sort the bills by earliest due dates

Make Breakfast

Plan out your day

It's time to check the mailbox today

You look out thinking it looks like it may rain today

As you open the mail you see a court envelope

You may are being evicted in ten days

Sunday you sulk about Monday. Monday you dread, but you grind like it's Tuesday, just to think about Wednesday. Reminiscing it's Thursday to cheer for Friday. Inspired by the weekend, Saturday you fill with errands. Only to extend the list to Sunday. Suppressing thoughts of reliving Monday, you wish Sunday stays a little longer then yesterday. The never ending cycle of wishing your life away.

Floating like a lily pad

I drowned in thought

I resurfaced for small breathes

from the potions of pond

I feel rested

I felt soft

Lilac colored my hair

Smelling like rosemary morning fog

Floating like a lily pad

Is all I ever wanted in the middle of this chaos

Our fingers travel globally in seconds

Our palms occupy first class seats

Accumulating infinite mileage points

Forcing us to forget working hard

Building brick by brick our lives

Relationships

and successes

With patience

Our expectations outweigh

Our level of understanding

We have become impatience instantaneously

It's not always your fault

Sometimes

I just make a mess out of nothing

I demand your undivided attention

I demand your applause

I demand your words

I demand your encouragement

I demand your respect

Upmost, I demand your dominance in places right below my spiritual healing

I demand

    I demand

        I demand

LOVE…

I will...

walk with you to the sun

    break concrete to help you build

        give you my lungs so you can breathe my air

            rust in coil mines to prevent you from being afraid

                disappear in space just to capture your
morning gaze

give my life so you can carry on your legend

    forget my maiden name just to become your best friend

stunt my growth

    sleep in desserts

    so you can thread an empire

I would do all these things without being asked

You just haven't noticed I'm a rare diamond

Covered

In mud

Silent Fears

First

The fear was loneliness

Second

Losing myself

Third

Losing you

Fourth

Learning love is nothing like a fairytale

Fifth

Trusting you loved me "unconditionally"

My apologies for needing a hug

Needing your warm hands to caress my face

Wanting to be held

Desperate to just converse

Communicate

My apologies for being too strong

Failing

To understand that it's ok to share this weight

For not knowing when to be an anchor

When to just enjoy the voyage

My apologies for wanting you in ways you may not want me

My mistake for thinking we shared our souls not just our flesh

In my mind

I'm stuck

Believing

Identifying

Destructing

Depicting

Rehearsing

Everything I am

Everything I'm not

Everything they told me I should be

In my mind I'm standing still

Pulling my knees close to my heart

Silently hoping I find the answers I need

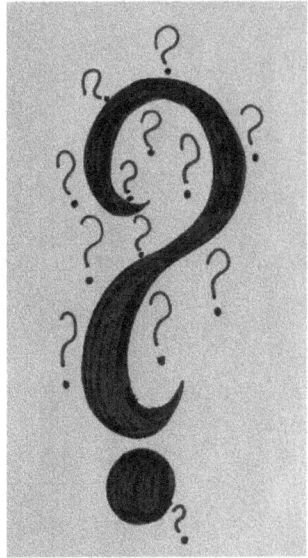

Blind Date

I'm checking his profile

I'm liking his recent statuses

I'm feeling his words of encouragement

I'm seeing he's single

Do I send him a friend request

Hoping he scrolls through my page

He doesn't know I've been dating his Facebook page

First Date

Shave my legs

Don't shave my legs

As if shaving my legs meant giving them permission

to sit closely or further apart

The shaver is my permission slip

I needed mom to sign

Taking Flight

Checking my engine

Leveling my fluids

    Review the checklist

Adjusting my mirrors

Intrigued by the written details in your manual

    We rehearse our manuscripts

Before propelling into the cockpit

Seduction

Wonder into the room with eyes that mirror my morning coffee

Grace my thoughts with the bite of your bottom lip

Invade my space with the smell of your fresh scent

Seduce me baby

Sit me down on your right knee

Have your eyes speak to me

Silently

I admire the ripples formed around your arms and spine

You are an epitome of chocolate delight

Seduce me baby

Break me open like the spine on novel books

Reach my walls with the tones of your deep voice

Whisper into my ear

"Let's tango blindfold"

You've seduced me

I can taste your seduction in my thoughts

Like I can feel myself gripping to hold onto this pen

Seasons Change

He felt like Spring

A seldom touch

Wet my lips

Whispered through my hair

Yanked on my skin

He felt like summer

Flushing my moist thoughts

With fingers rough as sand paper

He felt like autumn

Limbs like branches

I held on like leafs

He felt like winter

Awakened by loss

Cold sheets

Empty phone logs

Wifely Duties

Wash the dishes

Soak the clothes

Brush the kid's hair

Wipe their faces

Clean the counters

Vacuum the rugs

Will this long list of items ever shrink?

But you continue to move on

Cook dinner

Don't stop to think

Homework time with kids while he watches sports news week

You want to eat

Kids ask dessert mom or can we have a treat?

You ignore the rumbling sounds your tummy shrieks

You remember the work you must complete

But before you begin you send the kids to sleep

You seek silence, serene so you can think

Reading a book would help you unwind before the next day screams repeat!

Your body tired and full of agony

Down to your feet

Must now be open to please his company

You long for affection

A touch

A hello beautiful would be sweet

To help your heart skip a beat

Such a beautiful family to many you seem

No one sees the dry humor in the laughter you lost to routine

You no longer feel sexy

Sassy or sweet

You're simply the planner

The constant organizer

These are your wifely duties

Birthing Life

So many wonderful things about pregnancy and motherhood

From the first sonogram

To the first kick

To wondering will it be a girl or a boy

To who will the child look like most

Will it be healthy and smart?

You never thought you could love someone so much

Let's cut straight to the chase

Let us not forget

The times you broke out in your face

The pee you couldn't contain

The times you thought you farted but sharted instead

Yes, I walked around with shit in my pants blaming everyone except myself

Every time you poked your face your cheeks expanded at greater pace

You can't tell the difference

What's bigger, your ass or your waist?

But you smile at every belly rub to convince the crowd of your cheerfulness

MOLT

You wobble the halls

You search for cute clothes to help you feel beautiful with grace

You eat like you can't contain

You've had this unrolling hunger that just overpowers your strength

You check on your princess as she expands and darkens around every trace

As you weep knowing she won't ever look the same

You walk back and forth to exercise and escape

The thoughts of delivery that linger in space

You think of all the wonderful things of nursing and layettes

You smell every baby lotion bottle and envision your child's first day

Will it be sunny will it be born as the sun sets?

You never think about c sections, induction or hemorrhages you could face

You simply imagine the day you would see their face

It never dawns on you the great pain you and your child will experience

You simply want to get it over with so you can sleep facedown once again

Never do you ponder about the sleepless nights

The dark circles that will form on your face

The fact that your baby may not attach

That nursing could be painful and the least bit easy to maintain

You never even worry about the color variations going on between your neck, shoulders, and flabby waist

No one explained that once it's over a flabby piñata is what you would emulate

Now that it's over

Your baby is out

Your vagina is stitched together

Looking like a banged-up baseball in great need of tender love and care

Happiness will fade

As you doubt every part of your body

And your reasoning for this new stage

You find yourself taking longer bathroom breaks

Not because you really must go

Or you get to go when you want

I mean let us not elaborate

You're on the baby's time now

But the bathroom seems to be the only place

Where solitude and silence can animate

You try to gather your thoughts

with your head locked between your knees

trying not to lose your calm demeanor

As you return to the loud cries

Spit-up

And wondering how showering is a luxury

While he, your lover,

your reasoning for accepting this journey in the first place

Walks around naturally continuing life without a care and looking the same

It is his words of affirmation you long for at a steadier pace

God forbid a compliment from his mouth should escape

Inside he just wonders,

Is it your turn or his to change this poopy diaper that consumes the place?

Unwanted Delivery

The sun shines through the shades

My bedroom is bright filled with gleams

I've been sitting since four am quietly

Unable to sleep

I had chest pains

Belly pains

My feet I can't even see

It's only two weeks until the day of my delivery

My feet are swollen hovering over my shoe strings

Even my hands are tingly

I can't wear my sneaks

It's getting harder to breathe

I've dealt with gestational diabetes throughout this pregnancy

I hate pricking my fingers until they bleed

Something about knowing the needle will sting

I must do it four times a day

It's a daily routine

MOLT

I call the doctor begging and pleading

Something doesn't feel right

I feel sick and uneasy

They say I am thirsty

I need to drink more liquids she pleas

My blood pressure decreased from the last doctor I had seen

Three days later I feel overheated and weak

Painful and constant leakage after every time I pee

They say I'm not in labor because I'm not soaking pad sheets

I decide to visit my family doctor

I think she might be the key

As soon as I see her she says, "Go to the Emergency!"

My blood pressure was 144

I had blood in my urine

And spilling tons of protein

I panic because I was not ready to have my baby

At least not under these extremes

I pick up my older son from school

I call my husband and inform my family with the news

I arrive at the hospital scene

My blood pressure soared to a whopping 180

They decide to induce me so they can save me and my baby quickly

They break my water for me

I can feel the burst of water rolling past my knees

I think the worse is over

I believe the epidural is coming so I try to remember to breathe

At least in my mind is how I pictured this scene

The resident responsible of my delivery

Enters the room to inform me

My platelets dropped and I must deliver naturally

My only options are narcotics

And I panic and think how will this affect my baby

For a moment, I thought I could do it

I could do anything

I stare at the monitor beeping like it was the bible

And my baby's lifeline is being read by the ministry

My blood pressure is climbing

I panic and chose the narcotics

I can't take these painful contractions

They're coming too quickly

I can feel my hips beginning to crack

I feel an unbearable pain all over my body

My legs feel heavy

I'm just overwhelmed with fatigue and all I can do is scream

I start to ask God

Can I do this?

Am I too weak?

I've fought this hard I should see victory

The time has arrived

I need to push

Time to see him face to face

See what he looks like from head to tushy

Six minutes had passed

He has entered the world

But I don't hear his cries

His heart monitor never dropped

I know or I would've seen

He wasn't moving

He didn't see me

They take him away

Please God don't take my baby, I plead

I begin deep prayer as they continue to stitch me

Please bring me my baby

I need to see him, please?

After almost a minute he lets out a scream

All my hard work and this painful delivery

After kissing his hands, forehead and feet

It was forgotten shortly

It was a miracle

We both made it out clean sweep

Or so I thought

Horror was waiting at the seams

I was in for a rude awakening

145

145lbs is what I weighed when we first met

Your heart was beating 145 bpm

145cm tall was your big brothers height

four hours and 145 minutes of agony and excruciating pain I endured before seeing your face

145 seconds before I heard your voice

I almost lost you in room 145 on the day of your birth

In his eyes…

I'm a galaxy

I'm the northern star

I'm the sun that brightens his days

I'm the moon that graces the night

In his eyes…

I'm simply perfectly imperfect

I'm wise, smart and beautiful

I'm the anchor of this ship

In his eyes… I'm mom

The Mirror Lies too

I see the scars
form like
spider webs

Around my
belly button

They extend
their hands
around my
thighs

Just like
hanging
Christmas
lights

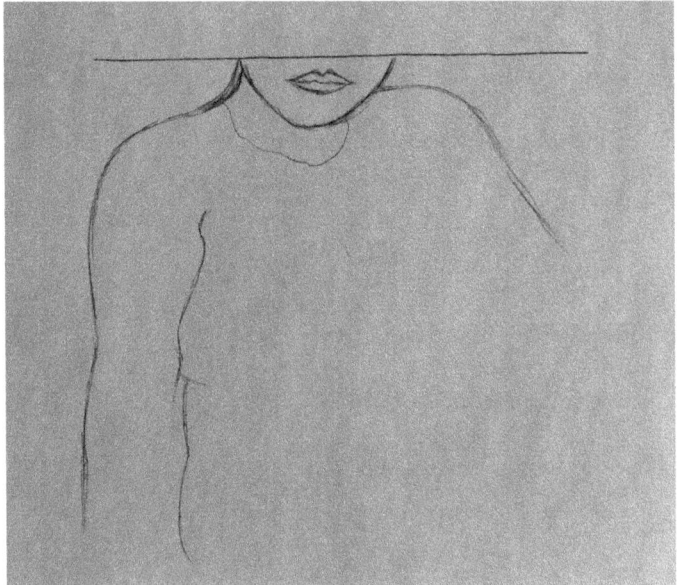

At first, I hated their synergy

I hated how thy crowded around forming allies against me

One day I took a closer look

They were gathering to form strength and love symbols

They are symbolic of a gift only women have been rewarded with…
Expanding Life

Motherhood

You expanded me in ways that I may never retract to being the same

You took my princess and left me with this fake imposter

You took all my good hairs and slowly replaced every other follicle with silver hairs

You filled my face and back with acne

Thank you, I always wished for those things

You sunk my mountains into dessert platoons

You postpone many opportunities to bogus late reservations

Soaking in the tub

The ability to read a book in peace

Can't even enjoy sexing without your screams

Rest you took that with you too

You fill me with glass ceilings because your stopwatch is impeccable, can't be a minute too late

I hate your guts when I think of all the puking I clean daily

All my cute blouses you've ruined with spilled milk and regurgitated baby food

Bathroom breaks must be scheduled too

You suck me dry of every ounce of energy

You're fucking exhausting to keep up with

I can't even make decent baked goods

You've taken my memory and replaced it with never-ending calendars, agendas and notes

I barely remember how to dress

Even worse I can't color coordinate

Wait, is showering too much to ask of you?

A date? Who needs one of those?

You've stolen all my money and reserves

You've taken my cute shoes and replaced them with flats and tennis shoes

You are the reason I hate to wear pencil skirts

I look like the eraser on top of pencil #2

Thank you, mean bitch!

And as much as I may hate you I love you, you're my best friend

I may not have time to beat my face but the gift you've given me puts the biggest smile on my face

My skin may be dry and my face painted with dark bags under my eyes

But I cannot picture my life without my boys

I cannot think without knowing they are safe

You have brought me motivation and a mean right fist

You helped me understand that I am superwoman

I can do anything

My uterus is stronger than any man's penis

Can you imagine a child coming out one of those things (a penis)?

Society would vanish, it might be one person on earth saying, "I exist"

For all these reasons, I hate you and I love you all the same

I'm sorry for my sporadic outbursts you can be a bitch that is hard to tame

Any Given Sunday

I wake up with God on my mental

I set my agenda to visit his temple

I open the curtains

Allow natural light to touch the dusty chairs and tables

I wash the dishes in the sink

I set the washer to color load and double rinse

I make breakfast for the family to feast

The baby begins to cry

Time to feed him before I can sit

I write down the grocery list

I wash and dress the children

Coordination and smell goods,

It's sort of a mom's thing

I glimpse at that clock

As it begins to tic

It's now past three

Oh no morning mass I've missed!

So, I ponder, sit back and think

Maybe I can make church this evening, it doesn't begin until six

Now it's my turn to shower and dress

But first I must make the choice

Wash this dirty mane or shave my hairy legs

Since I never have the time to do both

It's only a matter of time

Before the water turns cold

I guess the decision must depend

If sex will be an option of choice in the end

I must hurry up it's now a quarter to four

I still have dinner to fix

I stress as the car begins to get warm

I gather the kids

I pack up their things

It's now 4:30 and I haven't eaten a thing

My belly aches

Now I am hungry

But I decide to continue

And move on with the items on my listing

I've reached the grocery store

I unbuckle the baby

I carry him gently

I notice spit-up on my shirt and

To make matters worse

He's pooped and requires changing

I continue into the store to get the things I need

It is now 5:45 and mass begins in fifteen

I smell like spoiled milk

I feel defeated once again

So I breathe, drive away

Returning home, I'll try again next week, like I do every Sunday

Confident Queen

I am vintage and nobility

I'm not just some raggedy old thing you toy with endlessly

I am royalty mentally

Confidence resides in me

I am the key to building empires

I can wipe generations clean

It's time you started looking up to me

I can teach your daughters to wear their crowns properly

Confidence reigns in me

I have been abandoned by so many

It's as if you rather deal with peasants whose minds are empty

I'm a good woman, I can say that confidently

I finance myself I don't need your treasury

Don't waste my time, I take every minute seriously

I wear my bright heels with pride

I keep my head held high

I sit with my back straight

I walk the streets built for a king

Confidence is my attire regularly

Keep your distance if you cannot handle all of me

Not just when I am sweet

And when my waist is tiny

I don't just go along for the ride without knowing the direction of the journey

If your ego only has space for selfish delight

I rather you spare me from hearing your pathetic speech

I say this respectfully

I'm holding out for people just like me

Confident emotionally and spiritually

Confidence protects me from your negativity

Beauty is not defined by how large your backside can extend

Beauty is not defined by how high, large or small your size bra reads

Beauty is not just being cute in the face

And skinny at the waist

Beauty is not perfection

Beauty is not hidden behind eye pallets, bright lip shades, bright highlights that brightens your face

Beauty is knowing you are beautiful with every scar

Every mark

Every size or weight

It doesn't matter what age you are

Or what challenges you've faced

You are human perfectly imperfect

Don't try to change

Acceptance

Too many tears have been shed

Too much mental has gone to waste

Enough pacing in pity and trying to win the race

Misery you won't win

I'm done wondering

I'm over the hoping

The waiting

The deep thought and concentrating

I'm untying the ribbons

And claiming my mistakes

I am no longer stepping backward preventing my big break

I am extending my hand

Accepting my rewards with each trying day

I am putting on my armor to shield my wounded state

I will be remembered as a warrior

As I paint my face with confidence

I will enter the room with radiance as my dress

I will be the woman your daughters will love to address

I am not trying to become anyone's princess

I am grown

I am different from the rest

I am the legend my sons will propel and conjugate with their future Mrs. F

Going Invisible

Your womb expands and retracts like an accordion. You hold life in your hands while not recognizing your reflection. With each life, each push, each growing month; pieces of you subtract.

While you are beyond ecstatic at the thought of motherhood, the woman you once were becomes elusive. Your body begins to sway and hold up differently.

Your bosoms no longer stand with confidence. Your skin resembles quicken sand, pulling towards gravity. Your derriere sometimes leaves to later return or widens like a hand fan. Your emotions, moods, and sense of security play like ponies in the marry-go-round. Your skin forms different colored patterns and fall short of consistency in texture. Your nails fall and break off like leaves in the fall.

The glow of happiness and purity gets replaced with dark circles and heavy eyes. Rest you no longer sleep with. Your hair falls by the width.

Your memory... Well if you can remember what that is, has been swept away, wiped clean. Your sense of purpose slowly becomes undefined, understated and unachievable. You are mastering the art of going invisible.

Each day the mirror becomes the archenemy. You see this person, this human, and this once long ago confident woman, just starved and submissive to tyranny.

He (the man you love) no longer sees you as a desire. He only sees his food you cook, laundry you clean, and kids you feed. The greasy, spit up shirt you repeat. You simply become a number to text to check what's for dinner this evening? You are no longer the girl he once couldn't wait to see. You are no longer, good morning beautiful, good night love, or hey sunshine.

You are going invisible as a woman but growing more complacent in roles of secretary, nurse, psychologist, philosopher, tutor, confidant, friend, caregiver, chef, mom, and maid.

The woman you once were so confidently and proud is now standing inside the mirror trapped within a frame. This new unpredictably saddened, unhappy, unattractive, and quite frail woman has taken hold. You no longer understand what comes first; waking up to pee or waking up to nurse/feed the desperate cries of your newborn baby.

He who you once called lover, who made the hairs on the back of your neck stand up to attention. Whose voice made you quiver in your stance. Whose presence you desired deep in your loins, mind, body, soul. He who once made you leap for joy just from a kiss on the cheek. Who once was the prince you dreamed of so passionately to rescue you from the triumphs of adversity; enters the room to look passed you and focus on green paper.

Overtime becomes his favorite date. Sports are his old-time flings. TV is his new affair. The couch is his favorite girlfriend. ESPN is his favorite pass time.

Going invisible within his sight day by day as he masters fatherhood. Going invisible to your friends, as your phone resembles the dessert. Communication among your friends, your partner, yourself vanishes like boiling water to air. Going invisible in your spirit while still being physically involved. Going invisible in deep thoughts of doubt. You just roam the room, stuck in your insecurities, thoughts, aspirations, feeling defeated only to go unnoticed.

The color lipstick on your face, the eyeliner on your eyes, and the expensive foundation you never wear now defines beauty. To him and the kids you have became a mark on the calendar, a bullet point on the list, a task to be checked off, a visitor, a décor pillow that gets tossed around to make space, a spare for just in case, a blanket only for cold rainy days, an afterthought, a blank canvas stored in the basement corner, a secondary color to get mixed with the primary, a hardly ever used pocket watch, a vinyl record, an option instead of a priority.

You have gone invisible... Drowned in thought and emotion with no lifeguard on duty. Life continues outside your window even after you have gone missing inside, faded in appearance, and lost in the atmosphere. Someone will still yell out mom, babe for sex, and your legal name for work productivity. This is the act of going invisible as WOMAN.

20

A Predictable Ending

Some days are grand

Others are pure shit!

You love their little faces

But you wish you had a tractor to remove their screeching cries

You spend the day attending to their needs

Sun leaves and invites the moon to punch in

Now you think It's me time

You pour wine in a glass

Pick out a good book

Run the warm bath water

In minutes the bathroom smells like Rosemarie's

You insert your toes in the water

Before you can sit in your warm bath

Loud cries fill the room from the intercom

You wasted 10 mins and now you must return to the motherly duties

You settle the baby

Thinking you can now return to your calm serene moment

You insert your toes gently

Now the water is cold as ice

You try to take a sip of your wine

Only to taste a bitter after taste of rosemary bath water

You get upset

You feel like wanting time for yourself is an impossible task

You take a glimpse in the mirror

Notice your brittle dry hair

Your chewed-up nails

And your bushy ass eyebrows

Damn! No wonder you only wear hoodies and sweat pants

So, you take a typical 10-minute shower

Allowing the water to wash off the baby spit up from the corners of your curls

You breathe in disgust

For you hope tonight you can sleep

Without any interruptions

Maybe this is asking too much

Sometimes you feel like someone tied a rope around your neck

And it tightens up every 15 minutes

You feel like you want to escape to the nearest exit

You want to just ball your eyes out to remove the disgust and exhaustion

Your time is spent between the kitchen and changing table

It's like a never ending blind date with Huggies and Pampers

Any creative thought gets rudely interrupted

With cries followed by throw up

Even after your longest and hardest days

You love their stinky butts

You forget all of this when they fall asleep in your arms

Resembling angelic creatures sent down from heaven

No one would ever know how just moments ago you were a raging wild horse

Deuces Postpartum

I leaked Rivers

That later

The sun dried

I raised my head

To the clouds

And said

Make way, sunny days are ahead

Beating Postpartum Checklist

1. Know that everything will be ok.
2. Read number 1 again as many times as needed until you believe it.
3. You are still beautiful and attractive.
4. You're a bad momma jama!
5. Go on a date with friends or loved one. Leave the baby with a sitter so you can enjoy adult time.
6. It is ok to do things for yourself without the kids. It is necessary.
7. Take deep breathes. Fill your lungs with as much air as you can and let it out slowly. Repeat it again and again.
8. Don't feel bad about crying, you must let it out.
9. Breathe.
10. Sign up for a yoga or dance class.
11. If you can't nurse because you're ill, can't keep up with the baby, or simply hate it, know this secret, the baby will live. It doesn't make you a bad mom if you are unable to nurse your baby.
12. Go get your nails and hair done.
13. Buy yourself something that makes you feel nice and fuzzy inside.
14. Take long walks with the baby or with friends.
15. Breathe
16. Find a way to express yourself. Sign up for something you always wanted to try (photography, art, poetry etc.).
17. Read a new book.
18. Watch a comedy.
19. And when you feel like the world is closing in reach out for help.
20. It is ok, you're not alone.
21. Don't read any magazines or scroll through social media sites with people who look like models after just having a baby. You will get there on your own time.
22. If your funds are low because you have bought all the baby stuff, get a Groupon or have someone get it for you for something fun.
23. If you can't afford a gym membership, get free day passes to a gym with group classes.
24. Smile
25. Laugh at yourself.
26. Meditate as much as possible.
27. Everything and everyone will be fine.
28. You got this!

Strength of Women

We are beautiful no matter the flavor we're mixed with

Honey, coco powder, peanut butter or Vanilla

It makes us sweet in different ways

Our Strength, however

Is measured the same

We carry humans without lifting weights

We have battled thousands of moons

And under the sun we awake

Smiling each day

We have been beaten

Disrespected by everyone and everything

We have been caged under glass ceilings

The chains of heavy metal are locked to our feet

Eva ate from a tree

So, our children eat from rotten leaves

Still we keep pushing

Thriving

Without resting

It's the strength we share, we are legacies

Running Towards Something

Run like the wind

Jump like a grasshopper

Pull like an angry gorilla

Push through the pain like limbs in ice water

Dig deep

Fight your greatest enemy

"Self"

Only to look up and see the finish line pushed out further

Growth

Cheers

Sip on love like it's the liquid you need to travel your clogged arteries,

constipated intestines and into your cranky heart

Breach of Contract

Once I realized I was becoming your meal plan while you starved me of my energy, my sanity, and my natural ability to love

I cancelled the account permanently

The misconception is thinking you need a man

You want one

That's not the same thing

Narcissist

I was the fork, spoon, knife and dinner plate

Instead

You treated me like the saucer

Who only held your tea

Ready for our Duet

You ignite me

Like a lighter to your cigarette

You blow my brain

While holding me like a clarinet

You compose our song

With sharp and flat notes

You are the Nutella

I like to spread on my toast

Fellas

You claim you want a woman

Who supports your craft

Helps you build

Wipes your tears with understanding

Stands by your side when everyone goes missing

Fills every shoe no one could fit

That she's a real woman

Confident and radiant

Then she comes along asking for your

Heart

Loyalty

Time

And soul

You say she's too much for her keep

Then you wonder why you only get the girls who want bags and money

Feminism

One flower can be overlooked

But a bouquet of flowers draws the attention

Of everyone in the room

I've had a longer relationship with pain and hunger

Than

Love and opulence

Meeting him at the wrong time

Complicated was your status

Glamorous was my impression

Damaged was how we felt

Broken clocks are what we held

Husband…

I searched the world for you without having the slightest idea of who you could be

I glanced through many white ceilings

Silenced by hope and faith

I tried to find you in the faces I thought romanced me for love

Only later betrayed

I longed for you beneath the bright lights of many lonely moons

I cried and pleaded with the Universe for you under many cold showers

I fought myself for you so you wouldn't have to fight my wars

I begged that when you came I would be ready to be everything you ordained

I prayed for you more than I prayed for myself

I was lost because I gave so much power to a face I've never touched

A soul I have never met

I wasn't even sure you felt the same

A hopeless romantic just sitting behind windows from NYC to PA

I hoped you never felt this pain

Saddened by thoughts that you only existed in my brain

And once I let go

You walked into the room and told me your name

They say ghetto neighborhoods are scary

Clearly, they haven't visited the parenthood

Tuesday 5:02 am

I'm awake

Not due to some guys drunk text

      Or payment I didn't make

Instead

I look towards my husband

Whose snoring is insanely loud and in my face

I turn to the right to gaze at my first sons' bedroom

I check the monitor and see the baby sleeping

The house is quiet

Well

Besides the loud thunderstorms

I decided to type a page

But all that entered my head

Was

I've came a long way

My days may be chaotic

Every now and then

But I'm grateful for all

I am truly blessed

My heart fills with joy when I look over my family sleeping

I'm finally at peace

Now let's see if I can go back to sleep before they all awaken at the same time

Everyone loves stupidity because it makes you laugh contagiously and forget temporarily about pain

Science

Every great invention started out as some crazy theory

No one truly understands the impact of their creativity

Even the innovator fails to believe

They just changed the future they may not live to see

In all Seriousness

Being serious all the time is no fun

You have to make some bad decisions

You have to fuck up a few things

They make the best stories and

help you smile as you sit back to think

They were good times

They are good memories

Most inflated Cliché

"Do it this way "

Everyone Smiling is not Sincere

Some people laugh with a mouthful of veneers

They'll whisper toxins into your ears

They will make up stories about you to shatter your credibility

Simply because you're living a life they wish to adhere

Happiness

My heart skips a beat every time I hear you speak

When you gently kiss my cheek

I tingle inside like a girl whose found her favorite treat

And still I stare in disbelief

My heart drops to meet my feet

When your hands travel my physique

I relinquish control when you whisper sensual things into my ear

I die in your arms with just one peck on my forehead

I follow your guide as I hold your hand like my lifeline

I become woman

Free of compressed emotions

Open to engage

Only to awaken to finding white spillage gone to waste

I drained love into your veins

Only to be left empty

Alone and enraged

I gave you all of me to receive only a quick fix

Small satisfaction

Limited small doses of kindness wrapped in despair

I planned to stay with you

While your only intention was to visit

Pass by

Pretend to care

Wave hello and leave a spare

Audience

It doesn't matter the case I plead

My feelings were never a concern

I can beg and try to appeal to you in every way

It will never be about me

It's always about you anyway

People are hard to guide but easily mislead

Tabloids

I know you have a job to do

I know the stories must impress

I can understand

I can see the interest

What would trouble me the most if I was famous

Is that you told my story

Without checking on my progress

You told it your way

Instead of allowing me to decompress

I too have testimonies I wanted to express

Money doesn't give you consent to ruin my finesse

No one enjoys reading their private stories on magazines they didn't consent

Even though I am not in their shoes

I hate the context

The Healing

Healing begins when you've exhausted every feeling

You're drenched from all the tears

You feel trapped, alone in a corner in some unknown place

Your sun is hidden behind the gray clouds

You try to eat but can't find your appetite

You've reached rock bottom

But you pinch yourself repeatedly so you can feel something

Then when you have nowhere else to turn in this pitch-black room

You find a lantern and you light it

Morning… Sunday

There's something different about Sunday mornings

There's a calm serenity in the air

A natural soothing domineer about Sunday morning

Even the way you sip your coffee

Changes

The way the wind howls

The songs the birds chirp

Even the trees sway in a more romantically illusive way

Maybe it's the knowing

Maybe it's having faith

Having a feeling

God is staring through your window and waving shinny rays of changes through your curtains today

I know I couldn't leave a page out without speaking about faith and love for God. If you don't believe in God that is fine. I just hope you believe in something. So just humor me and repeat after me

God thank you for not giving up on me

If you would've given up on me every time I disobeyed you

I would've never made it this far

You have the power to wipe away the human existence

Move mountains

Create rainbows of miracles

Your love is unfailing and boundless

It is immeasurable

I know your love is not co-dependent on giving and taking

It's not about compromising or agreements

Instead, it is about acceptance and patience

You probably shouldn't love me this deeply

But I am glad you do

Please change in me these feelings of unworthiness

Change in me the feelings of emptiness and apathy

Remove the blinds that prevent me from seeing beyond what's in front of my nose

Forgive me for not loving you and trusting you more before

Thank you for keeping me in the midst of all these lessons and triumphs throughout my journey

Most of all thank you for listening and watching over me

Amen

By living in fear, you will never try anything for the first time...

If you've never been afraid

You've never left the nest and flown free

You may have missed the train to greater opportunities

My Sons

I will tear myself apart

I'll critique every decision I make

I'll doubt my abilities before anyone has a chance to see my masterpiece

But you are the one thing I know I did right

The only people who truly matter

Who view me with pure love

Without

Needing anything in exchange

Don't feel guilty about taking time for yourself

You are just as important as everyone else

Same Difference

The sun sets and rises

the

same

Everyday

Same color hues

Yet the sky is different

Every late afternoon

Character is what defines you

Reputation is what others make up to define you

Be careful to not allow reputation to define your character

You will get lost trying to read between the lines

Missing the silver linings

And trying to change the perceptions others think of you when you are unsure of your own reflection

It's ok to be somewhere in between

Accepting new upcoming changes

And

Wondering if you're doing the right thing

It only means you are evolving

You're growing into a better human being

Clouds don't wish on becoming trees

Trees don't wish on living in seas

If the universe accepts itself to simply be

Why waste time pretending

You are everything everyone can't be

You're blessed naturally

Sworn Secrecy

It's often been said that others cannot do to you what you do not allow them to

That is until they know your secrets

Your weaknesses

Your breaking point

Don't allow every landscaper you see work on your gardening

They may fertilize you with poison and make you believe its organic food

Bravery

Bravery is doing everything you want to do

It is setting goals that no matter the circumstances you achieve

It hates the life you wake up to so you invest in your dreams

Bravery is being vulnerable even when rejection is a possibility

It is walking into a room where others speak of you negatively and you stand in the center smiling confidently

Bravery is taking on every task even if you're unsure you'll complete successfully

It is risking everything for one thing… Inner peace

It is going to battle with demons without an army, simply because you believe in yourself so deeply

Bravery is being hurt but washing it away gently and watch it go down the sink

It is looking in the mirror and loving each scar, wrinkle, silver hair, and imperfections you see

It is knowing you're unhappy and choosing to do the unknown to live unapologetically

Bravery is loving everything even the past that cut you deep

It is knowing that when you lay yourself to sleep you lived every beauty of life

You felt every wind, you smelled every flower and watched the sun rise

You designed the rules and didn't allow anyone to seal you in their little box

I love dancing with words

If one ever gets tiresome

There's always another to fill in the right verse

Parents Letter

Mom and Dad, I know you worked hard to give me everything I needed

Dad may you continue to rest in peace

And I'm sorry growing up, I didn't know how sick you were getting

Maybe, if I would've visited and cared for you more I would've had the chance to say, "Au revoir, je' t'aime daddy"

I may never know how much of yourselves you both sacrificed daily

Even when times were hard

When we didn't have a large feast to eat

You both always tried to give me the best part of you, indefinitely

It took me sometime to understand

When you're young you wish you had everything like your friends

As a little girl wishing quietly that life would feel like warm sand and sunny beaches

I had no idea I was killing your joy little by little with comparison constantly

Now that I have children of my own I am grateful and hope I turned out at least close to what you planned

I didn't always agree

Sure, there are some things that could have been tweaked

I can now comprehend that the choices you made were based on beliefs

I just wanted you both to know I love you both abundantly

Thank you

I can never repay you for all you have done for me

Your Daughter, sincerely

You (I) Deserve…

You deserve a chocolate treat. You deserve a late night snack. You deserve to have a first language of carbs without feeling the need to translate to green. You deserve to drink wine from the cheapest to the debonair selection. You deserve to buy yourself nice things. You deserve to have caramel in your morning coffee or honey in your tea. You deserve, you deserve, you deserve…

You deserve to splurge on roses. You deserve to want more. You deserve that promotion you've been seeking. You deserve those shoes you've been saving up for. You deserve to go out with friends. You deserve to travel the world. You deserve a good man or girl. You deserve to be loved just as equally as you love someone else. You deserve to be hugged, protected, and told you are worth every fight. You deserve to know how beautiful or handsome you are. You deserve to wake up each morning feeling better than the person you were yesterday. You deserve… You deserve… You deserve…

You deserve to look in the mirror and feel gorgeous exactly as you are. To fall in love with every scar, wrinkle, mark, small or large features, mole, freckle, bump, patch, piercing, tattoo, and hairs on your precious body. You deserve to know that you are like morning coffee, exciting evening conversations, happy hour drink, winning game streak, new pair of jeans, fresh pair of shoes, new car smell, check deposit, late night ice cream, pancakes with syrup and confetti sugar, cheesecake on cheat diet day, morning run, promotion letter, laughter on the first date, I love you text, will you marry me… type feeling. You deserve everything your heart desires and so much more because you are worth "even though(s)." You deserve… You deserve… You deserve to read all of this again replacing (You) for (I) and actually believing what you just read.

Fresh Water Fish in The Ocean

When the tides are high

Keep S

    W

     I

    M

    M

     I

    N

    G

Take deep long strokes

Take short breathes

Reach the shore and yell to the clouds

I WILL NOT DROWN TODAY!

Poetry

I thank you for liberating me

I thank you for setting my mind free

I thank you for helping me find a voice I thought I'd never gain as a little girl

I thank you for being so liberal

For holding no grudges

For conveying no set rules

For making me understand that there's more than on way, shape or form, to express your love language

I thank you for keeping me when no one else would…

A New You

You can always evolve

You can always change

But it begins with intent

Before you have intent, you must sit next to change

Have dinner with your excuses and drink the wine of responsibility

If you miss this date you may never break the vicious cycle of stagnation

Letting Go…

Dwelling on what you don't have keeps you tied down to frustration

The fruits you grow will dry up sooner than quick sand

Set yourself free and remove the anchor of the past from your feet

Let that shit sink deep in the abyss of yesterday

Honest Conversations

I'd like to share something's with you if that's ok. I'd like to be completely honest with you now that I think we have gotten to know one another through this poetic journey. All these spilled thoughts and past thorns written on paper and still I struggle with the thought that you are reading these words. A part of me gets nervous and feels uneasy about sharing some of the most intimate parts of my life with you. You a total stranger, holding my spine, and finding relevance to stories dear to my heart I've struggled to even whisper in the wind. What puts me at ease is knowing that somehow, you and I, have reached common ground and peace, at least for a moment. However, I figured if you're going to be bold you might as well go all the way. Let me start by saying, Hi! My name is Astrid and here are a few things I struggle with that maybe you do too:

1. "Tell me about yourself?" Is probably my arch-enemy. I collapse in thought and go into instant brain-dead mode, because I struggle with, do I say too much or do I say too little? Do I tell them what they want to hear or do I tell them the truth? If I tell them the truth will they take me seriously? Will I pass this imaginary test of you are a person worth knowing? Or will I land the job? Does this happen to you too?

2. I have a hard time summarizing and keeping things simple when asked an opinion or thought. I am a big detail person. Ironically, when it comes to people I am not a detailed person. I sometimes think I was a man in my past life. I view things one way in my head. Problematic situations for example, I only think, tell me the problem and we can examine solutions. Let's skip the feelings part, the setting of where you were located, who you were with, and let's just brainstorm how you won't do this shit again!

3. I hate being wrong. Big surprise here!

4. Even though I am a Hispanic, I struggle hard with Latino slang. Let's be honest we use some terms that unless you been in the Monte (deep in the mountain trees) you will be dumbfounded. Sometimes it makes me feel like I am not Latina enough. Like I am a make-believe Dominican. Especially, when you are in the

Dominican Salons and those girls go in. If you go to the Dominican Salons you know what I am talking about. Think Barber Shop but with women speaking fast Spanish.

5. I am part Haitian and don't know a lick of Creole. You can blame my father.

6. Spelling and grammar (poorest grades on every school report card). The good ole days ha!

7. I do not like Yucca (probably get my Dominican card revoked for this one), and I am not the biggest fan of Salami either.

8. I do not have many friends not because I have problems making them, I am just not good at keeping them. I do not call, I may text here and there and I am very much type B, introvert personality. I figure, if something is up and you really need me, you'll call. I guess that's not a very good approach to have in friendships (insert I don't know emoji here).

9. I like to sit way in the back during public speaking events or classrooms, so I am never called to answer a question or volunteer. I'm more comfortable being part of the audience than the speaker.

10. I never recited poetry in public. Just the thought makes my palms sweat.

11. I still call every teacher Mr. or Mrs. Blah. Even if they're teaching my son. It feels like I am being disrespectful or doing a disservice if I don't call them by Mr./Mrs. Is that weird?

12. I had a low self-esteem growing up because I was always told I looked frail and skinny. I wished so hard one day I would have big breast and a big butt so that the boys would like me. Instead, I became a tom boy who was pretty much like one of the guys. Now I think it's one of the things my husband likes most about me. You know I like to think I am kinda cool, sometimes.

13. I often think I am the most boring person in the world. I mean, I enjoy being at peace by myself. I like simple things. Love fashion but I don't need to buy the latest and greatest. I am cheap as hell so I don't enjoy paying high prices for salads when I can have a big, juicy, mouthwatering, burger and fries for the same price. Sure, you can tell me I must work out all day to burn it off. Guess what? I'll still eat it.

14. I still struggle with what I should say in important conversations around successful people. I usually am very reserved because I am more afraid of saying something stupid. Or pretending to like a

sport that quite honestly, I am the worse person on the planet to have on your team, golf e.g.

15. I enjoy Disney movies more than I enjoy adult movies.

16. I wanted to become a ballerina when I was a little girl but my dad said, "HELL NO!"

17. I have a private affair with music. I have no problem dancing and making a fool out of myself in public. Maybe that is why I became a Zumba instructor.

18. I am always tripping over my feet and always look at the ground like it's his fault. I don't know why I haven't learned since I was five to be a little more careful planting my feet firmly on the ground.

19. Pessimistic is always my reaction when it comes to me personally, instead of being optimistic. Ironically, I am the first person to encourage someone else. I am always willing to give before I receive. Somehow, I haven't met many people who reciprocates that type of supportive attitude.

20. I hate arguments. I do not mind insightful, respectful and enlightening debates. I just don't enjoy giving closed minded people a piece of my energy. I rather save my energy for a good run.

21. I love children but I can't stay home with them. I rather be working than changing diapers all day. I know, I just said that. I love my babies but I need adult interaction. I'm just being honest. Stay at-home moms have the hardest job in the world in my humble opinion.

22. Finally, I love God with every fiber in my body. I feel he protected and shielded me through all my trials. I am a strong believer but I am not a person completely devoted to a church. I don't think that makes me any less of a believer or a bigger sinner.

Now I can say we have met. It's your turn. Tell me about yourself…

Dear Reader,

There were so many thoughts flowing through my mind

There was so much weighing on my heart

I hope my stories have helped and touched you in some way

Maybe it inspired you

Maybe it brought you some peace

Either way, thank you for taking the time to read my book of short stories and poetry

I know you could have chosen anything

You've allowed me the chance to share with you a large portion of me, personally

Now I feel light and ready to spread my wings

Thank you for this opportunity, I will cherish this moment for eternity

ABOUT THE AUTHOR

Astrid, born in Dominican Republic, and raised between the states of New York and Pennsylvania where she currently resides. She attended Kutztown University to obtain a Bachelors degree in computer science. After a year in Kutztown, she transferred to DeVry University where she graduated with a Bachelors in business information systems. Shortly after graduating, she decided to pursue her Masters degree in Business Administration at Keller Graduate School of Management. She was a single mother working full time while on her journey to obtain her masters degree. She graduated and continued her career working in the pharmaceutical industry. She is now a mother of two boys and happily married to her husband Jerel Ferguson, who is an up and coming artist in the Philadelphia region.

Astrid has always been a lover of poetry, music, and art. She faced many challenges growing up and found that through writing in diaries, and reading books from time to time was her escape. Now it has become a creative outlet she intendeds to sharpen each day. This is only the beginning of many projects she has in store.

www.ingramcontent.com/pod-product-compliance
Lightning Source LLC
LaVergne TN
LVHW091250080426
835510LV00007B/199